SPOTLIGHT ON
CIVIC COURAGE
HEROES OF CONSCIENCE™

AUNG SAN SUU KYI

BURMESE POLITICIAN AND ACTIVIST FOR DEMOCRACY

Alexis Burling

Rosen
YA™

New York

Published in 2018 by The Rosen Publishing Group, Inc.
29 East 21st Street, New York, NY 10010

Library of Congress Cataloging-in-Publication Data

Names: Burling, Alexis, author.
Title: Aung San Suu Kyi : Burmese politician and activist for democracy /Alexis Burling.
Description: New York : Rosen Publishing, 2018. | Series: Spotlight on civic courage: Heroes of conscience | Audience: Grades 5–10. | Includes bibliographical references and index.
Identifiers: LCCN 2017011080| ISBN 9781538380727 (library bound) | ISBN 9781538380697 (pbk.) | ISBN 9781538380703 (6-pack)
Subjects: LCSH: Aung San Suu Kyi—Juvenile literature. | Women heads of state—Biography—Juvenile literature. | Women political activists—Burma—Biography—Juvenile literature. | Women political prisoners—Burma—Biography—Juvenile literature. | Women Nobel Prize winners—Burma—Biography—Juvenile literature. | Democracy—Burma—Juvenile literature. | Burma—Politics and government—1988—Juvenile literature.
Classification: LCC DS530.53.A85 B87 2018 | DDC 959.105/4092 [B] —dc23
LC record available at https://lccn.loc.gov/2017011080

Manufactured in the United States of America

On the cover: This photo of Aung San Suu Kyi was taken on November 30, 2016, during a visit to Singapore. The photo in the background shows protesters in New Delhi, India, opposing the Myanmar government and calling for the release of Aung San Suu Kyi on May 30, 2006.

CONTENTS

A Hero for Democracy

For much of the twentieth century, Burma—now called Myanmar—was one of the most oppressed countries in the world. After years of seeking independence from British occupation, the newly sovereign country was ruled by a military dictator accused of horrible human rights abuses. Millions of Burmese people went without food or adequate shelter.

But despite their dire state, the Burmese had hope. It came in the form of a woman who they believed could bring about positive change in Myanmar. Her name is Aung San Suu Kyi.

For three decades, Suu Kyi risked her life to work as an advocate for the Burmese people. But she didn't have it easy. She spent more than fifteen years under house arrest. Still, her efforts didn't go unnoticed. She was awarded the Nobel Peace Prize in 1991. In 2016, she was elected to one of the highest government positions. Because of her courageous vision and groundbreaking accomplishments, Aung San Suu Kyi became a symbol of freedom not only for people in Myanmar, but for those around the world.

For more than thirty years, Aung San Suu Kyi has been an outspoken leader in Myanmar's prodemocracy movement. This photo is from her 2014 visit to the Brandenburg Gate in Berlin, a national symbol of peace and unity in Germany.

BURMA'S DIVIDED PAST

In the twenty-first century, Myanmar was finally on the road toward democracy, thanks to Aung San Suu Kyi. But for many centuries, the country was a battleground for different ethnic groups. Bordered by China to the north, Laos to the east, India to the northwest, Thailand to the southeast, and Bangladesh to the west, Myanmar is the second-largest country in Southeast Asia.

Settlers first arrived in the area nearly eleven thousand years ago. Starting around 200 BCE, peoples such as the Pyu and the Mon in the south and the Burmans in the north formed city-states. There were also many rural communities. These minisocieties practiced a variety of cultural traditions, but most were Buddhists. Buddhism advocates giving up worldly pursuits to search for enlightenment.

In 1057, King Anawrahta became the first leader to unify the disparate ethnicities under one Burmese empire, with Pagan as its capital. From that point forward until 1886, new ruling dynasties emerged, including the Ava (1364–1527); the Toungoo (1531–1752); and the Alaungpaya (1752–1885).

Pagan (now called Bagan) is an ancient city in central Myanmar. It is one of the richest archaeological sites in Southeast Asia, with more than two thousand sacred temples and Buddhist shrines.

The Burmese Empire grew to be one of the most powerful monarchies in Southeast Asia. Because of this, it needed to protect itself against foreign interests. Burma was full of valuable resources, such as teak and rubies. Other countries also wanted access to its valuable trade routes between China and India.

In 1885, England waged war against Burma for the third time and won. The British exiled the Burmese king, annexed northern Burma as a colony, and made the entire country a province of India, with Rangoon as the capital.

Burma suffered under British rule. Farmers lost their land. British missionaries imposed Christianity in schools, and Buddhists monks were no longer permitted to participate in government. The traditional Burmese economy collapsed.

Circumstances within the country became so desperate that the Burmese people rebelled. Beginning in the 1920s, a group of students joined the protests and formed the nationalist Thakin movement. The Thakins were led by a man who would later steer the country toward independence: Aung San Suu Kyi's father, Aung San.

Around 75 percent of the world's teak comes from Burma's forests. Under British occupation, elephants hauled teak logs to waterways for export. The wood was also used to build British ships.

A Legacy of Activism

W hen Aung San Suu Kyi was born in Rangoon on June 19, 1945, her country was two years away from becoming a sovereign nation. Her father, thirty-year-old Aung San, had been fighting for the nationalist cause for more than fifteen years, first as a student organizer, then as a general during World War II, and finally as deputy chairman of Burma's Executive Council. Aung San had become a symbol of freedom for the Burmese people.

On July 19, 1947, when Aung San Suu Kyi was still a toddler, tragedy struck. Political rivals stormed into the council chamber in Rangoon. They opened fire, killing Aung San and six other cabinet members.

Aung San Suu Kyi and her older brothers, Aung San Oo and Aung San Lin, were left without a father. The Burmese were without a leader. Yet despite the loss, Aung San's efforts were not in vain. On January 4, 1948, Burma won its independence. It was a turning point that Aung San Suu Kyi looked back on many times in the years to come.

General Aung San was a revolutionary who founded the Burmese army. He also started the Communist Party of Burma and engineered Burma's independence from the British. He was assassinated in 1947.

Inspiration from Her Mother

Aung San Suu Kyi grew up with only a distant memory of her father. But in her mother, Khin Kyi, she found a role model who was equally devoted to bettering Burma. In her book *Freedom from Fear*, Suu Kyi wrote, "From my earliest childhood my mother taught me this idea of national unity; not by merely talking about it but by including it in everyday work."

Khin Kyi accomplished extraordinary feats beyond what was expected of a Burmese woman. She served as the director of the National Women and Children's Welfare Board in Burma's parliament from 1947 to 1952. She was elected chairperson of the Social Planning Commission in 1953. In 1960, when Suu Kyi was fifteen, Khin Kyi moved the family to India and became her country's first female ambassador.

Because of her mother's position, Aung San Suu Kyi was exposed to influential people in India, including Prime Minister Jawaharlal Nehru and his daughter, the politician Indira

Aung San Suu Kyi (*front center*) attributes much of her success to her mother. Khin Kyi (*left*) was a devoted wife to Aung San (*right*) and a doting mother to their children.

Gandhi. Suu Kyi also blossomed into an avid reader and a hardworking student. Her intelligence and diligence proved to be the key to her success in college and beyond.

STUDIES ABROAD

After attending Lady Shri Ram College at the University of Delhi, in India, for two years, Aung San Suu Kyi continued her education at St. Hugh's College, at the University of Oxford in England. According to her classmates, she didn't succumb to the popular freewheeling attitudes of the 1960s. Instead, she remained dignified and proper at all times. She graduated with a bachelor of arts in philosophy, economics, and politics in 1967.

Two years later, Suu Kyi was accepted to a postgraduate program at New York University. But after moving to the United States, she was offered an equally prestigious opportunity she couldn't pass up. Putting her studies on hold, she took a job as the assistant secretary for the Advisory Committee on Administrative and Budgetary Questions at the United Nations. There, she worked with some of the world's largest human rights organizations. It was an experience that would influence her political outlook in the years to come.

From 1964 to 1967, Aung San Suu Kyi attended St. Hugh's College, at the University of Oxford, in England. Founded in 1886, St. Hugh's admits around eight hundred students and has both undergraduates and graduate students.

FORMING A SACRED BOND

Aung San Suu Kyi was extraordinarily dedicated to her work. But she was also preoccupied by thoughts of Michael Aris, a handsome man she had met while studying at Oxford. While Suu Kyi was working in New York, Aris was in Bhutan studying Buddhism and tutoring the royal family. They corresponded regularly by letter.

Eventually, Suu Kyi and Aris could no longer stand to be apart. On January 1, 1972, they married. Suu Kyi left New York and moved to Bhutan to be with Aris. She got a job as a research officer for the Royal Ministry of Foreign Affairs.

In 1973, Suu Kyi and Aris relocated to London. They had their first son, Alexander. Three years later, they moved to Oxford, where they had their second son, Kim. Suu Kyi adored her new family. In addition to being a mother, she continued to pursue academic

studies. She traveled to Japan as a visiting scholar at Kyoto University's Center for Southeast Asian Studies, partially to research her father. In 1984, Suu Kyi published a biography of the famous general.

Kyoto University is one of the top educational institutions in Asia. In 2016, Aung San Suu Kyi returned there to receive an honorary doctorate for her ongoing commitment to freedom, democracy, and human rights.

A Changed Landscape

Before Aung San Suu Kyi and Michael Aris got married, they wrote nearly two hundred letters to each other. Suu Kyi expressed her desire to return to Burma, even though she feared being separated from the man she loved. In one letter she wrote, "I only ask one thing, that should my people need me, you would help me to do my duty by them."

In 1988, both her fear and desire were realized. Khin Kyi suffered a stroke and Suu Kyi returned to Burma alone to care for her. When she arrived, she found a different country than the one she had left when she was a teenager.

Since 1947, General U Ne Win's Burma Socialist Programme Party had wrested control of the government and ruled with an iron fist. Ne Win's socialist policies—nationalizing land and industry—were failing and the Burmese people were suffering. By the summer of 1988, protests had hit a peak. Though Ne Win resigned in July, Burma seemed on the verge of revolution.

General U Ne Win, seen here, was the first military commander to become prime minister of Burma. In 1962, he stole control of the government out from under then prime minister U Nu.

Aung San Suu Kyi's Vision

Aung San Suu Kyi's return to Rangoon in 1988 was a fortuitous one. The Burmese people were in need of a leader they could trust and Suu Kyi was the perfect candidate.

On August 26, Aung San Suu Kyi made her first public speech in support of the prodemocracy movement and the need for a multiparty system, as well as free elections. She spoke of her father's influence and her goal to create a society in which all citizens benefited and the country's disparate ethnic groups could coexist in peace.

Over the next month, Suu Kyi led nonviolent protests throughout the country and amassed thousands of supporters. But on September 18, armed forces led by General Saw Maung seized control of the government and replaced it with the State Law and Order Restoration Council (SLORC), with Saw Maung as chairman and prime minister. SLORC violently suppressed the demonstrations, and thousands of

On September 19, 1988, thousands of Buddhist monks throughout Burma joined in peaceful protest against the government. They carried flags and signs. Many were arrested, murdered, or fled to neighboring countries.

unarmed protesters were killed. Another dark period in the history of Burma had begun.

Under House Arrest

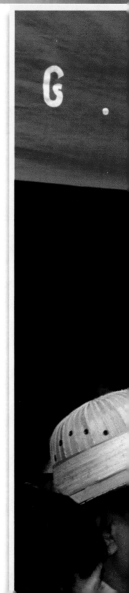

In December 1988, Khin Kyi died. Despite her loss, Aung San Suu Kyi remained determined to speak out against the ruthless government. She wrote letters to international human rights organizations like Amnesty International and the United Nations, asking for help. She also cofounded the National League for Democracy (NLD) and was appointed the party's general secretary.

Suu Kyi's reputation continued to grow. But because of her opposition to SLORC's policies, she paid a steep price. In July 1989, Saw Maung's government put her under house arrest. Armed guards were posted outside her home in Rangoon. She had little access to the outside world, including to her husband and children, who were back in England.

Suu Kyi was offered the chance for freedom if she agreed to leave the country for good. She refused.

Instead, she remained sequestered for the next six years, biding her time by meditating, reading the teachings of peace activists Nelson Mandela and Mahatma Gandhi, playing piano, and listening to news of Burma's increasingly untenable political situation on the radio.

In the months before Aung San Suu Kyi's first term of house arrest began, she toured Burma and gave fiery prodemocracy speeches to audiences of more than ten thousand people.

FROM BURMA TO MYANMAR

During Aung San Suu Kyi's first term of house arrest, a number of important changes took place in Burma. Under Prime Minster Saw Maung, SLORC officially changed the name of the country to Myanmar. The name of the capital was also switched from Rangoon to Yangon. The name changes were controversial, and many within Burma and around the world did not use the new names.

In May 1990, Myanmar held its first multiparty elections in thirty years. Many groups participated, including the current military government's National Unity Party (NUP) and Suu Kyi's opposition party, the NLD. Saw Maung was confident that his party would win. However the NLD prevailed in a landslide victory, winning 392 out of 485 seats in Parliament. SLORC refused to recognize the election results. Instead, leading members of the NLD were imprisoned and SLORC continued to impose increasingly violent and oppressive measures against the Burmese people.

On May 27, 1990, Burma held general elections. Under the watchful eye of representatives from each political party, election officials counted the ballots on the floor of a public school in the nation's capital.

Prodemocracy supporters in Myanmar and around the world were outraged. So was Aung San Suu Kyi. Despite the risks, she vowed to continue to do whatever it took to bring justice for her country.

BREAKING HER CHAINS

By the early 1990s, Aung San Suu Kyi's plight had attracted the world's attention. She received the prestigious Sakharov Prize for Freedom of Thought in 1990. In 1991, she was awarded one of the greatest honors of all: the Nobel Peace Prize. Since she was still under house arrest and couldn't attend the ceremony in person, her son Alexander accepted the award in her place.

"Suu Kyi's struggle is one of the most extraordinary examples of civil courage in Asia in recent decades," read the Norwegian Nobel Committee's statement. "She has become an important symbol in the struggle against oppression."

Finally in 1995, Suu Kyi's term of house arrest ended. Upon her release, she picked up where she left off six years earlier. Aris and her sons immediately came to visit. Despite the government's attempts to keep Suu Kyi silent, she staged more rallies around the country. Her courage and resolve were stronger than ever.

On December 10, 1991, Alexander Aris (*center*) accepted the Nobel Peace Prize for his mother, Aung San Suu Kyi, who was under house arrest. Kim Aris (*right*) also attended the ceremony.

By 1997, the human rights violations in Myanmar had reached catastrophic proportions. More than twenty thousand refugees from Myanmar fled to neighboring Thailand as a result of SLORC's military offensive against the Karen National Union, the last remaining ethnic group refusing to cooperate with the government.

In response, the United States invoked economic sanctions against Myanmar and restricted contact between the two countries. The European Union followed suit.

To appease foreign leaders, SLORC allowed the NLD to hold its party congress for the first time since Aung San Suu Kyi had been imprisoned. But their next move was back to the old formula. On November 15, SLORC reorganized into an even more brutal military-backed government called the State Peace and Development Council (SPDC) and threw hundreds of NLD party members and supporters in jail.

The following year, Suu Kyi retaliated. In September, she and other NLD members formed a committee they claimed was the country's legitimate ruling parliament. According to their directions, all SPDC laws were to be ignored.

On January 4, 1997, NLD opposition leader Aung San Suu Kyi gave a speech to hundreds of supporters to mark the forty-ninth anniversary of her country's fight for independence.

A GRAVE SACRIFICE

Aung San Suu Kyi was making headway in the movement toward democracy. But in 1999, she encountered a significant setback. Her husband sent word from England that he had been diagnosed with a terminal form of prostate cancer. He didn't have much longer to live.

Aris applied for a traveler's visa to visit his wife in Rangoon (now Yangon) but was denied. Suu Kyi was faced with an agonizing decision. She knew that if she left the country, the government would refuse to let her back in because of her political activities. She chose to stay in Myanmar.

Michael Aris died on his fifty-third birthday, March 27, 1999. The last time he had seen his wife was during Christmas in 1995. During his lifetime, he had become a renowned scholar on Tibetan and Himalayan studies, taught at Harvard University, and published many books. He even edited *Freedom from Fear*, a collection of essays, speeches, and interviews written and given by his wife.

Despite their separation, Michael Aris was firmly devoted to his wife and her mission. Until his death in 1999, a large photograph of Aung San Suu Kyi hung above his bed.

International Demand for Release

Over the next decade, Aung San Suu Kyi was put under house arrest twice more because of her efforts to unseat the military government—from September 2000 to May 2002 and from 2003 to 2010. During the interim period, an assassination attempt was made on her life, but she escaped. The government was suspected of being behind the attack, but no one was formally charged.

In 2009, widespread international outrage at Suu Kyi's circumstances prompted the United Nations to declare her detention illegal under Myanmar's law. But just as she was scheduled for release in May of that year, she was arrested and charged with violating the terms of her house arrest for receiving a visitor at her compound. She was convicted. Her three-year sentence was later reduced to eighteen months, which she served, once again, under house arrest.

All told, Suu Kyi spent fifteen years isolated from the public. Despite that, she didn't flounder. In fact, she was more

On June 19, 2009, Burmese demonstrators held up posters with portraits of Aung San Suu Kyi in New Delhi, India, during a protest to mark the opposition leader's sixty-fourth birthday.

dedicated than ever to fighting for democracy and human rights in her country.

AN ELECTION IN MYANMAR

Just days before Aung San Suu Kyi was freed in 2010, elections were held in Myanmar. A new constitution adopted in 2008 stated that a quarter of each legislative chamber would be appointed by the military leadership.

The constitution also decreed that any person married to a foreign national or convicted of a crime would be banned from running for office. Suu Kyi had done both. Many of her followers believed that this was the government's attempt to squelch her power and prevent her from running for office.

To show their support for Suu Kyi, the NLD refused to participate in the rigged 2010 election. The party was stripped of its political rights. Consequently, the military dictatorship was once again victorious. Widespread voter fraud was suspected.

After Suu Kyi's release on November 13, government leaders did their best to pretend she didn't exist. They suppressed mentions of her in the press and ignored her calls for reform. Despite the huge crowds that followed her wherever she went, the government hoped in vain that she would somehow disappear.

On November 14, 2010, thousands of prodemocracy supporters greeted Aung San Suu Kyi at NLD headquarters in Yangon upon her release from house arrest.

A MOVE TOWARD REFORM

N ow that she was free, Aung Sang Suu Kyi had no plans to willingly withdraw from the public eye. A third of her country lived below the poverty line. Thousands of dissidents were still in jail. Health care and education received only 2 percent of the country's budget, compared to the 40 percent reserved for the military.

But change was afoot. In March 2011, Thein Sein was sworn in as president of a new, ostensibly civilian government, ending fifty years of brutal military rule. That November, the NLD reregistered as a political party, with Suu Kyi running at the head for a seat in Parliament. After a grueling campaign, she won in 2012 and served until 2015.

During those three years, Suu Kyi accomplished a great deal. In an unprecedented move,

she traveled outside the country and met with prominent world leaders to restore relations, including US secretary of state Hillary Clinton and President Barack Obama. She helped abolish the government's censorship of the Burmese media and negotiated the release of thousands of political prisoners.

On November 19, 2012, President Obama became the first sitting US president to visit Myanmar. He and Secretary Clinton met with Aung San Suu Kyi at Suu Kyi's residence in Yangon.

THE LADY'S GLOBAL APPEAL

By 2015, Aung San Suu Kyi had spent most of her adult life fighting to unify her country and bring peace and prosperity to her people. She had made great sacrifices in order to do so, including giving up the ability to spend time with her family and watch her sons grow into adults.

But the world had noticed. The United States awarded her two of the highest honors for her work. She was given the Presidential Medal of Freedom by President Bill Clinton in 2000 and the Congressional Gold Medal in 2008 by President George W. Bush.

After being thwarted at almost every turn, she was finally given the chance to lead at home. In Myanmar's November 2015 parliamentary elections, Suu Kyi's NLD party won in another landslide victory. Unlike in 1990, the results were uncontested. Though she was still constitutionally barred from becoming president, Suu Kyi was appointed state counselor in April 2016. It was a position many believed would allow her to rule "above the president" until changes to the Constitution could be addressed.

As state counselor, Aung San Suu Kyi travels throughout the world to negotiate new alliances with prominent powers. On August 19, 2016, she met with officials in Beijing, China, to boost diplomatic ties.

Aung San Suu Kyi, whom many call "The Lady" because of her dignity and grace, continues to serve as an inspiration to people across the globe. Though she has been criticized in recent years for her supposed indifference to the plight of the Rohingyas, a Muslim people living in camps in western Myanmar, Suu Kyi has done much to follow in her beloved father's footsteps.

In addition to always striving for an ever-freer, more equal Myanmar, Suu Kyi has been an outspoken proponent of human rights. One of her many recent endeavors includes acting as a global advocate for zero discrimination with the Joint United Nations Programme for HIV/AIDS.

Most of all, Suu Kyi is an embodiment of courage in the ongoing fight for change. "If we want democracy, we need to show courage," she wrote in *Freedom from Fear*. "By courage I mean the courage to do what one knows is right, even if one is afraid."

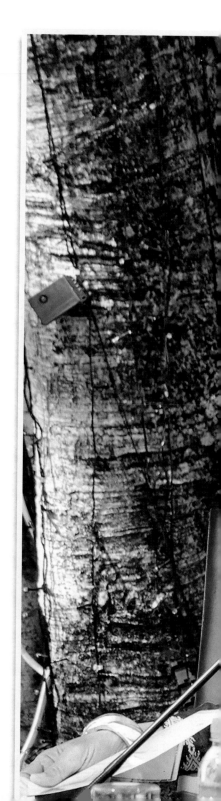

On February 12, 2017, Suu Kyi spoke at the Panglong Peace Conference, which was organized in an attempt to help stem the violence between the Myanmar army and armed ethnic groups in the country's Panglong region.

GLOSSARY

annex To add land to an existing state or country.

appease To do something, especially something you don't want to do, to make others happy.

catastrophic Terrible; disastrous.

disparate Different; not similar.

dissident A person who disagrees with a commonly held or approved-of belief, often for political reasons.

ethnic Characteristic of a group of people who share a common homeland, culture, or religion.

exile To send someone away permanently, especially from his or her home country.

fortuitous Lucky or fortunate; happening by chance.

house arrest When an arrested person serves his or her prison sentence at home.

oppressed To be abused or kept down by a more powerful group, such as a government.

ostensibly Supposedly; outwardly appearing as so.

plight Circumstances, usually an unfavorable situation.

prestigious Very well respected.

prosperity Success, especially in the form of wealth.

refugees People who run away or are trying to escape from a dangerous or unsafe place.

ruthless Cruel.

sanctions Penalties against a country or group, usually economic.

sequester To separate, remove, or hide.

sovereign Independent and self-governing.

succumb To give up or yield to.

terminal Deadly.

unprecedented Never done before.

untenable Shaky; out of one's control.

Asia Society
725 Park Avenue
New York, NY 10021
(212) 288-6400
Website: http://asiasociety.org/new-york
Facebook: @asiasociety
Twitter: @asiasociety
Instagram: @asiasociety
YouTube: @Asia Society

The Asia Society is a leading nonprofit educational organization dedicated to strengthening partnership opportunities and fostering an understanding among peoples, leaders, and institutions throughout the United States and Asia. Its Center for Global Education partners with schools, parents, and community members to provide educational opportunities for students to help them better prepare for a global-centric future.

Canadian Museum for Human Rights
85 Israel Asper Way
Winnipeg, MB R3C 0L5
Canada
(877) 877-6037
Website: https://www.humanrights.ca
Facebook: @canadianmuseumforhumanrights
Twitter: @CMHR_News
Instagram: @cmhr_mcdp
YouTube: @Canadian Museum for Human Rights

The Canadian Museum for Human Rights is the first museum in Canada solely dedicated to examining the evolution, celebration, and future of human rights in the country and throughout the world. Visitors are invited to explore ten core galleries and two rotating exhibits pertaining to fighting hate and oppression throughout the world.

Dayton International Peace Museum
208 West Monument Avenue
Dayton, OH 45402

(937) 227-3223

Website: http://www.daytonpeacemuseum.org

Twitter: @peacemuseumohio

The Dayton International Peace Museum is dedicated to teaching the public about peaceful solutions to the world's most pressing problems. Its permanent and rotating temporary exhibits aim to help people of all ages learn nonviolent responses to conflict. An interactive children's room on the second floor allows kids and teens to play, participate in discussion groups, and learn about other cultures.

Human Rights Watch

350 Fifth Avenue, 34th Floor

New York, NY 10118-3299

(212) 290-4700

Website: https://www.hrw.org

Facebook: @humanRightsWatch

Twitter: @hrw

Human Rights Watch is a nonprofit, nongovernmental organization dedicated to fighting human rights atrocities around the world and advocating for changes in policy in order to promote justice for impoverished or otherwise marginalized people.

WEBSITES

Because of the changing nature of internet links, Rosen Publishing has developed an online list of websites related to the subject of this book. This site is updated regularly. Please use this link to access the list:

http://www.rosenlinks.com/CIVC/Kyi

FOR FURTHER READING

Baptiste, Tracey. *Nelson Mandela: Nobel Peace Prize-Winning Warrior for Hope and Harmony*. New York, NY: Britannica Educational Publishing, 2016.

Caldwell, S. A., Clare Hibbert, Andrea Mills, Rona Skene, and Philip Parker. *100 Women Who Made History*. New York, NY: DK Children, 2017.

Cooper, Alison. *Facts About Buddhism*. New York, NY: Rosen Publishing, 2011.

Harris, Nathaniel. *Burma (Myanmar)*. New York, NY: Cavendish Square Publishing, 2010.

La Bella, Laura. *Aung San Suu Kyi: Myanmar's Freedom Fighter*. New York, NY: Rosen Publishing, 2014.

Lowenstein, Tom. *The Civilization of Ancient India and Southeast Asia*. New York, NY: Rosen Publishing, 2012.

Lucas, Eileen. *Mahatma Gandhi: Fighting for Indian Independence*. New York, NY: Enslow Publishing, 2017.

Mara, Wil. *Myanmar*. Danbury, CT: Children's Press/Franklin Watts Trade, 2016.

O'Keefe, Sherry. *Champion of Freedom: Aung San Suu Kyi*. Greensboro, NC: Morgan Reynolds Publishing, 2011.

Perkins, Mitali. *Bamboo People*. Watertown, MA: Charlesbridge Publishing, 2012.

BIBLIOGRAPHY

Aung San Suu Kyi. *Freedom from Fear and Other Writings.* New York, NY: Viking, 1991.

Aung San Suu Kyi. *The Voice of Hope: Conversations with Alan Clements.* New York, NY: Seven Stories Press, 1997.

Beech, Hannah. "Aung San Suu Kyi: Burma's First Lady of Freedom." *TIME*, December 29, 2010. http://content.time.com/time /magazine/article/0,9171,2040197,00.html.

Burma Campaign UK. "A Biography of Aung San Suu Kyi." BurmaCampaignUK.org.uk. Retrieved February 27, 2017. http://burmacampaign.org.uk/about-burma/a-biography-of -aung-san-suu-kyi.

Emont, Jon. "Is This the Real Aung San Suu Kyi?" *New Republic,* December 22, 2016. https://newrepublic.com/article/139476 /real-aung-san-suu-kyi.

Hammer, Joshua. "A Free Woman." *New Yorker,* January 24, 2011. http://www.newyorker.com/magazine/2011/01/24/a-free -woman.

Hammer, Joshua. "Aung San Suu Kyi, Burma's Revolutionary Leader." *Smithsonian*, September 2012. http://www.smithsonianmag .com/people-places/aung-san-suu-kyi-burmas-revolutionary -leader-17728151.

Pederson, Rena. *The Burma Spring: Aung San Suu Kyi and the New Struggle for the Soul of a Nation.* New York, NY: Pegasus Books, 2015.

Snowdon, Peter, and Katie Inman. "A Profile of Aung San Suu Kyi." *The Documentary*, BBC World Service, November 9, 2015. http://www.bbc.co.uk/programmes/p037khxn.

Wintle, Justin. *Perfect Hostage: A Life of Aung San Suu Kyi, Burma's Prisoner of Conscience.* New York, NY: Skyhorse Publishing, 2007.

INDEX

About the Author

Alexis Burling has published numerous books and articles for kids and teens on a variety of topics ranging from current events and career advice to how to get the most out of reading nonfiction. She specializes in writing biographies, particularly those of courageous women like Aung San Suu Kyi who have changed the course of history despite incredibly daunting odds. One day she hopes to travel to Myanmar to witness Suu Kyi's positive influence on her country. Burling lives with her husband and cat, Suki, in Portland, Oregon.

Credits

Cover (portrait) Suhaimi Abdullah/Getty Images; cover (background) Manan Vatsyayana/AFP/Getty Images; p. 5 360b/Shutterstock.com; pp. 6-7 happystock/Shutterstock.com; pp. 8-9 Popperfoto/Getty Images; p. 11 Pictures from History/Bridgeman Images; p. 13 Kyodo News/Getty Images; p. 15 Oxford Picture Library/Alamy Stock Photo; pp. 16-17 TK Kurikawa/Shutterstock.com; p. 19 Keystone/Hulton Archive/Getty Images; pp. 21, 25, 26-27, 31 © AP Images; pp. 22-23 Dominic Faulder/Camera Press/Redux; p. 29 David Van Der Veen/AFP/Getty Images; p. 33 Raveendran/AFP/Getty Images; p. 35 Getty Images; pp. 36-37 Official White House Photo by Pete Souza/flickr.com/photos/obamawhitehouse/8248705110/in/photolist-dyULDC; p. 39 Pool/Getty Images; pp. 40-41 Aung Htet/AFP/Getty Images; cover and interior pages stars pattern f-64 Photo Office/amanaimagesRF/Thinkstock.

Series Designer/Book Layout: Brian Garvey; Editor: Amelie von Zumbusch; Photo Researcher: Nicole DiMella